# SMASHING

## *Brooke Berman*

**BROADWAY PLAY PUBLISHING INC**
224 E 62nd St, NY, NY 10065
www.broadwayplaypub.com
info@broadwayplaypub.com

SMASHING

© Copyright 2010 by Brooke Berman

First printing: June 2010
Second printing: March 2011
I S B N: 978-0-88145-434-5

Book design: Marie Donovan
Typographic controls: Adobe InDesign
Typeface: Palatino
Printed and bound in the U S A

SMASHING was developed at The Eugene O'Neill Theater Center in Waterford, CT, and with M C C Theater's Playwrights Coalition.

SMASHING received its world premiere by The Play Company. The cast and creative contributors were as follows:

ABBY ......................................................... Catherine Powell
CLEA ......................................................... Merritt Weaver
JASON ............................................................ David Barlow
JAMES ............................................................ Joseph Siravo
NICKY ......................................................... Lucas Papaelias

*Director* ...................................................... Trip Cullman
*Set design* ..................................................... Erik Flatmo
*Costume design* ............................................ Michael Krass
*Lighting design* .............................................. Paul Whitaker
*Sound design* ................................................ Scott Myers

# CHARACTERS

ABBY
CLEA
JASON
JAMES
NICKY

# NOTE

This play takes place in three very distinct levels and time-frames. The first is the present reality. The second is the fictional world of the book. The third is the past. These areas should be clearly indicated in the design or lighting of the play, so that it is clear when and where we move. Also, Jason should have some sort of podium or "reading" area when he reads from his book.

Everything speaks their text very well and very accurately. Use the language as a driving force. The play should move very quickly with no break between scenes. Everything happens on top of itself. It is a rhythmic, hypertext influenced structure. Characters speak directly to the audience, narrating themselves, and acting as the "link" on a website. The text of Jason's book may be wound through or looped in a soundscape.

All of this is intentionally theatrical. The characters love to perform, and the act of telling is a major part of the story itself. In a very active and literal sense, the telling is the story. These characters, writers all, use language as a weapon, an instrument to manipulate in order to get attention and sustenance. Embrace the act of telling.

"I think I've unconsciously chosen people who are emotionally crippled, who need mothering. I'm really good at it, and it mirrors something in me that needs mothering."
Madonna, *Truth or Dare*


"I wanted to make people happy, I wanted to be famous, I wanted everybody to love me, I wanted to be a star. I worked really hard and my dream came true."
Madonna, *Truth or Dare*

# ACT ONE

## overture

*(The stage is bare. Enter* JASON STARK, *an average looking, skinny, writer. He reads from his novel:)*

JASON: Book Number One. Jameson Addie. The Girl.

*(Lights up on* ABBY MEADOW. *A beautiful thin girl in her very early twenties. A student. She is rational, gutsy and self possessed.)*

ABBY: Every day you can wake up new. There's nothing permanent about the self. "Reality" either.

*(Add* CLEA, ABBY's *best friend, slightly rougher around the edges, marches to a different drummer. Also twenty-one. Obsessed with two things—Madonna and* ABBY.)

CLEA: Says my best friend Abby—

JASON: Says the Buddha through the mouth of Jameson Addie.

ABBY: It's always shifting.

CLEA: At least, this is the position put forth by numerous schools of thought, mostly coming from the teachings of the Buddha. Abby says:

ABBY: Impermanence is key.
  Nothing's fixed—except your projections in the moment, which is eternally now.

*(Lights up on* JAMES MEADOW, *a charismatic novelist and* ABBY's *dad.)*

JAMES: It's called *Eternally Now*. Which is a comment on one of my earlier novellas, *Now, Eternal*. The new piece uses a character from *The Eden Trilogy* and takes him into the far reaches of Bhutan; it's the last Buddhist kingdom in the Himalayas.... You see, I should probably mention that my daughter went to India this past year and I started to think about, see kids are just great for bringing up ideas because they're basically search engines.

ABBY: So every day you can wake up new.

CLEA: It's summer now.

ABBY: Without attachment or projection.

CLEA: She's back at her dad's brownstone, sleeping late. I work in Admissions. And in the evenings, we meet.

ABBY: No past, no future, nothing holding you to who you were a day ago, an hour ago—

JASON: She will always be sixteen. She will always be The Girl.

ABBY: Except—

JASON: Beautiful. Smashing.

CLEA: And here is the exception.

JASON: "With a mean streak. A talent for hurting, for hitting, for driving a stake. At least that is how I remember her, this vicious Jameson Addie. I remember her wet. Dripping. Sixteen and mean. Out for blood. Out for my blood. And I remember liking it."

ABBY: The exception is if you fucked some guy when you were sixteen and he wrote a book about it and this book is roughly everywhere. I mean, if some asshole you slept with when you were like basically still in

high school writes a best-selling book all about your
pussy and what a bitch you are and reveals things
to the world, aren't you kind of forced into being
someone you got through being a long time ago?
    If a tree falls in the forest—

CLEA: And it's reviewed by *The New York Times*, by *The
New York Review of Books*, by *People* magazine even—

ABBY: If actresses you don't like at all are considering
doing the movie, well, you're just stuck with this
projection, aren't you?


## jason is a hero, to himself

(JASON *talks about himself like he's a superhero.*)

JASON: In the fabulous cities of the New World, the
Young Writer Jason Stark reads from his fabulous
new book. *Cherry Pie @ the Hungarian*. The young
writer Jason Stark, the celebrated young—okay, so
I'm twenty-nine but I still get grants for "emerging"—
writer is on his American book tour, giving readings,
attending cocktail parties, answering "questions"
about his second book because he has a three book
deal—only he's preoccupied. Thinking only of her.
Wondering if he will run into Her, The Girl. He
sees the ghost of her sixteen-ness everywhere, on
every subway, at every bookstore and every café.
But she misses her entrance. She (Deliberately? He
thinks, deliberately due to the revealing nature of his
scandalous debut) refuses to be seen. And he returns
to London—that's right, London—the city where he
makes his Young Writer Home—ready for Books
Number Two and Three. But what are Books Number
Two and Three going to be about? Norman Mailer
says that writer's block is a failure of the ego. Yeah,
well my fucking ego is fucking failing. I kind of said it

with Book Number One. Love turned sour. Fucked up fucking with sixteen year old muse/tornado/Lolita-girl—

(ABBY *cuts him off before he can say her name.*)

ABBY: Abby. Abby Meadow. Once it was Medowski but my dad, the famous novelist James Meadow changed it when he was a hippie and my mom, whose name was originally Daphne changed hers to Dandelion or something that sounded like that in French, she was French, well she died when I was a little girl, yeah, it's okay, I mean I'm fine about that, but anyway, I'm sixteen and kinda running wild, alone in the house when you come, this guy working for my dad. Who's just not around much that Spring and Summer. But you, Jason, are around. Doing whatever it is you are being paid to do. Which is not, I gather, to crush out on the daughter of your boss.

  You read me poems.

JASON: e e cummings.

  "inane, the poetic carcass of a girl"

ABBY: And we have sex—

JASON: Mad passionate sex—

ABBY: —all over my dad's black leather writers chair while he's in Prague. My dad says Prague's his favorite city. And we fuck on his chair. A lot. And then I break your heart, which just really can't be helped, and you go away.

JASON: Until now.

### she touches things and they move

CLEA: Madonna Marathon. Three whole days of nonstop Madonna on your favorite music video network. One must stay in for events like this. One must ferret out the people one knows with television sets and cable. To absorb all the imagery surrounding Her. The most famous woman in the world. Self-made, self-invented and totally self-serving. Unapologetic. Fierce. A goddess. She touches things and they move. She shifts and the culture shifts with her. She gets everything right, even when she's wrong. Clearly, she is my hero. I mean, she would be if I believed in that kind of thing, which I don't because Abby says they break your heart, but if I did, she'd be it. She helps me persevere in the face of great odds. And a girl alone in college in New York City with an insufficient Pell Grant and an overdeveloped inner life does face these odds. Rather a lot. But She walked this path before me. Alone in the City without resources. Getting into the groove.

(*Scene. The girls watch VH-1.*)

ABBY: She's all about herself.

CLEA: So?

ABBY: So, that's ego.

CLEA: So? (*Beat*) I mean, don't you think that's a bold statement? She's not self-effacing. Or self-punishing. And her drive is like, you know, we should support drive. And blonde ambition.

ABBY: Sure. But for good causes. Her cause is just, herself.

CLEA: Not true. She does a lot for AIDS groups and— she totally raises money for AIDS groups. Besides, some people have to get themselves out of a bad place and into a better one before they can be like, a statement for larger forces.

ABBY: Maybe.

CLEA: I took this religion class last semester where they said that the sacraments were conceived on this totally patriarchal model and that for women it's a different thing altogether. I mean, like, for us, anger and drive and ambition, all that stuff female characters always get totally punished for? Those might be our sacraments.

ABBY: What class was this?

CLEA: Women and Religion.

ABBY: I see.

CLEA: It was a good class.

ABBY: I'm sure. *(Changing the subject)* Hey, do you want this stuff? *(Points to a bag of clothes)* Just isn't me anymore. Maybe you'll find something.

## abby at sixteen

JASON: Jack Kerouac says the girls in Iowa City are the prettiest in the whole damn country. But what does he know about it? He was passing through in a hot rod car with Dean Moriarty. He never had to live there. No, no. Jack was Jack and I was Jason, someone else entirely, and I couldn't wait to get to New York. The girls in New York, especially the ones who grew up there, are my favorite in all the world. Abby at sixteen. My favorite in all the world.

*(She becomes* ABBY *at sixteen. There is a shift indicating we are now in the past, or possibly the novel.)*

JASON: Short for Abigail?

ABBY: I wish. I had weird parents.

JASON: *Absalom, Absalom?*

ABBY: Not Faulkner. You didn't really think...

JASON: I was joking.

(ABBY *twirls a little, flirting. She, everything about her, already mesmerizes* JASON.)

ABBY: So you wanna know what it is?

JASON: Sure.

ABBY: Absinthe.

JASON: Really?

ABBY: That's what's on the birth certificate. Ask my dad.

JASON: Wow. Mine's just Jason. Like, I don't know. I think I was named after someone on a soap opera.

ABBY: My dad's a freak.

JASON: Your dad is my hero.

ABBY: That's stupid.

JASON: Why is it stupid?

ABBY: It just is.

JASON: His books changed my life.

ABBY: Which ones?

JASON: The Eden Trilogy.

ABBY: Yeah. They're pretty good. Still though. I don't think you should have a hero. Heroes are dangerous.

JASON: Why's that?

ABBY: They break your heart. They just do.

JASON: How old are you?

ABBY: Sixteen.

JASON: Wow.

(ABBY *smiles. They share a moment. Danger, Will
Robinson.*)

CLEA: Abby and I have been friends since the first day
of school. Her house is AMAZING. Life is good when
you get invited to the brownstone. They have these
dinners all the time with writers and artists, and you
never know what poet you'll meet or who will tell you
embarrassing things about their love lives and rehab
experiences, and what things were like in "the Factory
days". They talk about "movements" in literature and
culture. This is very different than where I come from.
I listen. I take it all in. I absorb. I don't say a word. If I
talk, they'll notice me, and they may ask me to leave.
And I can't leave. I have too much at stake. A whole
life. Waiting and at stake.

(*This is broken as* JASON *returning to the present, picks up
his novel and reads*—)

JASON: Her name was Addie, though on the birth
certificate it said "Jameson". But this was no Jamie,
no Jan, she was Addie short for Jameson, because she
liked it and she had always been allowed to do as she
liked. She was named after her father's favorite drink,
a drink he liked when he was young, an expatriate
hippie, but he was old when I met him, when I met
them both, and she was just Addie. For addiction,
addled with guilt, address the problem. A dirty little
girl with a truck driver's mouth and the face of a
saint. A poor little rich girl. The daughter of a literary
legend—

## james is a famous writer

JAMES: *(As if lecturing to a class) The Eden Trilogy. Eternally Now. Daphne/Delphine,* that one's about my wife who died very young. *Genius in the Heartland. A River in the Sun. Grass in the Blade.* That's my personal favorite, though I didn't care much for the movie adaptation. I mean, I just didn't understand some of the casting. But, you know, the movies. They seem to take great pleasure in getting things wrong.

*(To* JASON*)*

JAMES: I was wondering if you could do me a favor.

JASON: Sure.

JAMES: Good. I'll pay you extra if you can hang out with my daughter, keep an eye on her.

JASON: Like baby-sit?

JAMES: Just keep her busy. She's fairly self-sufficient. But I travel quite frequently, and it would help me out a lot if you'd be willing to "like baby-sit," as you call it, while I'm away. Just keep an eye on her. She's a great kid. Smart. Doesn't eat much. Knows all those writers you like. A good editor, too. You can show her what you're working on. Take her to a movie here and there. On me. I'd appreciate it.

JASON: Sure. I don't mind at all.

*(The scene switches almost immediately as* JASON *turn to* ABBY, *and—)*

### abby at sixteen, carpe diem and all that

JASON: Your dad said to keep you busy. Want to go to a movie?

ABBY: Do you want to kiss me?

(JASON *maybe stammering*)

ABBY: You do, don't you? I know. You've been looking at me like that all week and it's making me sort of impatient. So, I think you should just do it. Carpe Diem, and all that. *(She waits.)* Well?

(JASON *makes no move to kiss* ABBY.)

ABBY: Come on. Just fucking kiss me.

JASON: Not when you put it like that.

ABBY: Fine.

(ABBY *kisses* JASON. *He kisses her back. It's good.*)


### the things you are missing

CLEA: When Abby was in India, I took notes. So we'd be on the same page when she got back. *(She opens a notebook or journal.)* The Things You Are Missing (This starts out lame, but gets better) *(She looks at her notes, then begins.)*

Coffee prices increase at University Food Market.

Kissed Nietzsche Surfer Guy *(finally)* in front of Avery library. Not memorable. Followed by Hungarian Pastry. Also not memorable. Really wish I could call you. You'd say this is not a sign of things to come, and frankly, I hope you are right.

Okay, this is interesting. Went to Times Square to see "The Next Best Thing" and—well, it's disappointing but she looks great. Only she's talking like a Brit. Do you think is a conscious appropriation for some meta-purpose we don't yet understand? You'd say no, but I might disagree.

Nietzsche Surfer Guy has defected to the Dark Side. He's dating Barbie Girl. It's a mess. Again, *really* wish I could call you.

Oh. Started writing my first short story. Or novella. It might be a novella. It's about this girl Louise. Louise has a best friend, Veronica, who's the center, the absolute center of—everything—

Anyway. I never read the list to Abby.

## obsession is a perfume, not a way to live your life

JASON: I call. I'm drunk. It's late. But who can sleep when you're on the verge of fame but have nothing to say in books number two and three? And you need to talk to the inane carcass of a girl you wrote about and loved and loved and got hurt by and wrote about. (*He picks up the phone—*) Is it you, Pretty Girl? Inane Carcass?

(ABBY *answers the phone. Stage goes split screen.*)

ABBY: Jason?

JASON: Have you seen it?

ABBY: Seen what?

JASON: The book. Have you seen the book?

ABBY: Uh-uh. What book?

JASON: What book? My book?

ABBY: You have a book?

JASON: You don't know about my book?

ABBY: No. Where are you? Are you in New York? I thought you were, like, weren't you living somewhere else?

JASON: My book got published. It's huge. There was a piece in the—I'm in London.

ABBY: What are you doing in London?

JASON: Didn't you get the letter?

ABBY: No. You wrote me a letter? What did you say?

JASON: I can't believe you didn't get the letter.

ABBY: Well. I didn't. I was in India. Traveling and stuff. Did you send it to my dad's? Cause he's been away too. Or school? Traveling was amazing, it was just amazing, I saw all these—

JASON: You were supposed to get my letter.

ABBY: Yeah, well I didn't. I was traveling. In India. Wait, can you hold on? That's call waiting—

JASON: Abby, I am calling you from London. England. I cannot just hold on—

ABBY: Okay, hold on. *(She clicks flash)* Yeah?

CLEA: Hey. What's wrong?

ABBY: Oh, God, just come over.

CLEA: Why?

ABBY: Remember that guy I told you about who I slept with when I was in high school while my dad was in Prague?

CLEA: Yeah?

ABBY: Well, I'm on the phone with him, so just come over.

*(Overlapping, they speak "just come over" at about the same time)*

CLEA: Okay, I'll just come over. I'm at the deli. You want anything?

ABBY: No. Yeah. Diet Coke.

CLEA: No, bad for you. Aspartame. It actually creates this insulin release effect in the body which then subsequently makes you crave—

ABBY: Fine. I gotta get back to this weird guy. He's weird.

CLEA: Weird how?

ABBY: Obsessive.

CLEA: Dangerous?

ABBY: No. Just obsessive. Okay, I gotta get back to him. Just come over.

CLEA: (*Aside*) Things like this happen to her all the time.

(ABBY *clicks back to* JASON—)

ABBY: I'm back—

JASON: So I have to write another one.

ABBY: So write another one. What did you say in this letter?

JASON: You don't understand. They want me to write another book.

ABBY: Yeah. You said.

JASON: Well, I can't just do that.

ABBY: Why not?

JASON: I don't know.

ABBY: Why are you calling me?

JASON: You really haven't read the book? You didn't even notice it? It's huge. There are movie rights— I have a three book contract—

ABBY: I told you. I was in India. Do you want to hear about India? India was—

JASON: Chloe Sevigny wants to play...the girl.

ABBY: What's the girl like?

JASON: It's getting good reviews.

ABBY: What do you want from this conversation?
I mean, it's not like we're in touch—

JASON: I just want to talk to you.

ABBY: Well, you're talking to me.

JASON: I just, I can't, I mean, it's great, and I'm really
lucky, it's just that now with this contract and—you
know they want me to write—and I just—

ABBY: Oh. You have writers block. Deal with it. My
God. Writers are so self-indulgent.

*(The following occur simultaneously—overlapping to the
public school line, then overlapping again until ABBY breaks
it.)*

JASON: *(Sparring, liking it)* Don 't—

ABBY: WHY ARE YOU CALLING ME, JASON?

JASON: I mean, you just—that's like reductive, just
because,

ABBY: I don't really want to talk to you. Or have you
yell at me, okay?

JASON: *You're* yelling at *me*!

ABBY: I mean, there are poor people, I have seen people
in India—

JASON: Yeah whatever with your "poor people in
India" you were just this white tourist anyway and
it's not like the poor people in India give one rat's ass
about—

ABBY: I mean, you are just this totally over-privileged, I
mean, freaking out because you have a book contract—

JASON: Look who's calling who over-privileged. *I went
to public schools you know.*

Just don't call it "writers block" like it's this totally
pat ordinary thing—

ABBY: WHATEVER. (*Breaking the simultaneity*) You
called me. Why did you call me? Right before you
picked up the phone, you probably had a thought
about something. What do you think it was? Try to
remember—

JASON: Well, I didn't go and call it "writers block"
That's so dismissive.

ABBY: I'm hanging up.

JASON: No. Don't go. Nothing is happening in my life
besides being a writer, Not even writing, just being a
"writer". And, I'm sure that, I'm having these—I can't
write, I think about you all the time. And I need to see
you. Okay? I need to see you.

ABBY: You want to see me?

JASON: Need. Not want. Need.

ABBY: Oh.

JASON: I just think that it would help me right now. I
think I'd write again. There. Okay? There. I just need to
see you, Abby.

ABBY: Well. You're in London.

JASON: Come here.

ABBY: I can't—

JASON: You're my good luck charm.

ABBY: That's dumb.

JASON: It's not. Why is it dumb?

ABBY: It just is.

JASON: You're my muse. Is that dumb?

ABBY: You haven't seen me in—a long time. Years.

JASON: Yes. That is the point. That is the whole point exactly.

ABBY: Yeah. That *is* the point.

JASON: I have a picture of you in my mind. Do you think about me? Ever?

ABBY: No. I'm sorry. But, no. I never think about you.

JASON: You're lying.

ABBY: Maybe. Okay, so maybe I think about you. So? Maybe every now and then. But not a lot. I mean, I do not think about you a lot.

JASON: You recognized my voice.

ABBY: You called me "inane carcass".

JASON: So? Come here. Please? I want to see you. I want to touch you. I'm a novelist. Don't you want to see me be a novelist?

ABBY: I grew up with novelists. I don't need to see another one.

JASON: *(Direct, not pathetic)* I'll beg. Want me to beg?

ABBY: No.

JASON: Where are you right now?

ABBY: In my apartment, Jerk-off, where do you think I am? You called me.

JASON: I know. But. Tell me where you are. So I can see it. Describe it to me. The room, what you look like...

ABBY: Jason, I'm not having phone sex with you. Go fuck yourself.

JASON: Come here.

ABBY: I'll think about it. Okay? I will think about once I've read your stupid, pathetic little book. Where can I get it?

JASON: Anywhere. You can get it most anywhere. There was a piece in the—It's huge.

(*Somewhere during this sequence* CLEA *enters, silently, carrying her bag from the store. She tries to interest* ABBY *in water or some non-aspartame-based soft drink,* ABBY *shakes her head no,* CLEA *listens, silently to rest of conversation.* ABBY *and* CLEA *gesture to one another in appropriate moments.*)

ABBY: Great. Are you happy? You should be really happy.

JASON: I'm still in love with you.

ABBY: No you're not.

JASON: : I am, though. You're the only thing that makes me want to write.

ABBY: Thing?

JASON: Look. Okay, I'm older than you—

ABBY: Not that older—

JASON: And at my age, my friends have had relationships that were good and then went bad. And, they're ready, this makes them ready for the one that works. And I think, it's you. Okay? The good one. I think it's you. For me. You're old enough now. It wouldn't be weird. Your dad's out of it. What if we had, or even tried...? What if it's You?

ABBY: Jason. It's not me. It wasn't me then. And it isn't me now. Go find someone in England. There are plenty of girls in England.

JASON: I want you.

ABBY: You don't want me.

JASON: Don't tell me what I want. I do. I want you.

ABBY: I say this with great compassion. Go fuck someone in England and write about them. It's what my dad does when he can't think of what to write.

JASON: Yeah?

(JASON *considers this. It is a worthwhile option....* ABBY *hangs up.*)

(ABBY *and* CLEA *share a moment.*)

ABBY: Obsession is a perfume, not a way of life.

CLEA: Too bad he's not dangerous.

ABBY: No, not dangerous. Just obsessive.

CLEA: Obsessive?

ABBY: Yes. And there's a book—

## a book about being numb

JASON: —about pain. It is a book about pain. About being numb and then waking to pain. You are numb, then you are shocked into awareness and once you're aware, you are aware of pain. You were perhaps in pain all along but you were numb so you didn't feel it. Anything. You didn't feel anything. This is what the book is about. And the catalyst for all of this is The Girl. The Girl is really important because she is the Thing that shocks the Guy into awareness.

## a dangerous hobby

CLEA: We make heroes. We can't help it. We kill our heroes. We make words about them. I'm only just starting, and let me tell you, it's a dangerous hobby.

### on fancy stationery from london

JAMES: (*Reading a letter*)

Dear James,
No doubt you have seen my best-selling debut *Cherry Pie @ The Hungarian* which in my mind, if not in print, I dedicate to you and all you taught me. You are my literary hero, and although it has been said that heroes are dangerous and break one's heart, I am writing to you in hopes that you will read my book and possibly review it for a special feature on writers and their protégées...

### reading said book

(JAMES *holds a copy of* JASON's *book. The cover is obscured, perhaps it is a "review copy" —in any case, not yet the picture of* ABBY.)

JAMES: Have you seen this book?

ABBY: No.

JAMES: Do you know what it's about?

ABBY: No. What's it about?

JAMES: I think it's about you.

ABBY: Me how?

JAMES: You naked.

ABBY: Really? How strange.

JAMES: I'm going to pretend it's fiction.

ABBY: Yes. I'd do that.

### abby meets addie

(ABBY *buys the book. She stands at a bookstore. There is an enormous display poster of a young girl with mousy blonde hair and fishnet stockings. She is a cross between Lolita, Eloise at the Plaza and an Egon Schiele drawing, hair tousled, black stockings or knee highs, skirt around her ankles. This is the cover of* JASON'*s book. The girl looks exactly like* ABBY.)

(*Somehow, either through gesture or design,* ABBY *becomes the poster image—as if, she morphs into the version of herself that appears on the cover of this book. It is a specific physical pose, ripe with innuendo—Jameson Addie. She holds this pose long enough for us to feel the impact of this fictional character—*)

(*Then, she becomes herself again.*)

ABBY: Oh. Fuck. It's about me.

### abby, clea, the book

ABBY: I can't read it alone.

CLEA: Of course.

ABBY: Stay.

CLEA: Of course.

ABBY: Oh.

CLEA: What?

ABBY: He didn't.

CLEA: What!?

ABBY: That motherfucker—

CLEA: What!?

ABBY: He wrote about me.

CLEA: You knew that.

ABBY: I didn't know how.

CLEA: How?

*(And the book goes:)*

JASON: "...tormenting me, making me ache...selfish,
self impressed...her literary references covering her
fear of fellatio, I never got to see her empty selfish
meaningless face suck my cock...give me head, you
selfish selfish selfish bitch...."

*(ABBY looks up from book, horrified. Both girls turn back to
the text reading more. It is a bad dream.)*

JASON: ...her mom died leaving her alone in an empty
house full of books...with an egomaniacal father who
worshipped her and left her alone to rot, ignored her,
adored her...set me up to fuck her because he couldn't
do it himself. No wonder she was such an easy lay,
wide open, she was wide open, waiting. She had been
prepared for it..."

ABBY: A lot. He wrote about me a lot.

*(And once more,)*

JASON: At least if she'd sucked my cock, I'd have
something to remember her by. The image of her face,
my—"

*(ABBY and CLEA girls discard the book entirely.)*

CLEA: Wow. He's mad.

ABBY: Clearly.

CLEA: You dumped him, right? He's mad that you
dumped him and not the other way around.

ABBY: It wasn't like that. Like how he says. I can never
go out.

CLEA: It's a revenge novel.

ABBY: Ever again.

CLEA: People will think he made it up.

ABBY: Her name is Addie. Her dad's a writer. Author of *Three Books of the Apple*. Her mom is dead. She fucks this guy in her dad's black leather chair. Her hair is the color of bones. I mean, it's me.

*(Addie, the poster girl, hovers nearby, grinning.)*

ABBY: Clearly it's me.

### james on whiny prose

JAMES: I should mention here that I wrote about my first love. Years ago. Her name was Isobel, and we both worked at the Public Library in Brooklyn when I was young and saving money for Columbia. (The school, not the country.) I wrote about her, every detail of our tragic affair, something about fucking her near the stack containing Hemingway's *The Sun Also Rises*, but I have not published this piece of work. The prose whines. You can tell when the prose itself does this, whines.

So, the Isobel stories remain unpublished in a drawer.

### all geography

ABBY: Look. It was all geography. He was in my house. And I liked him enough. Enough to lose my virginity, enough to spend, I don't know, maybe five months, six, fucking his brains out behind my dad's back.

CLEA: I see.

ABBY: He was...I didn't know anyone from Iowa. It was exotic.

CLEA: I'm from Michigan. It's not very far away from, well, I guess it is from Iowa because there is Illinois, you see, not to mention Wisconsin, and—

ABBY: I was really young. And he loved me. I mean, I didn't think about it too much, but, of course he loved me, I was me, and he was like this older guy, twenty-four, skinny, a grad student, kinda strung out or something. Shy. It wasn't like in that book.

## what it was really like:
## jason and abby five years earlier

ABBY: You're shy.

JASON: Is that bad?

ABBY: It is if you want to kiss girls. We like you to make the moves.

JASON: How do you know so much?

ABBY: You can't kiss and talk at the same time. Pick one.

(ABBY and JASON kiss.)

JASON: Here. I'm giving you this.

(JASON hands ABBY a book

ABBY: Oh, I know him. He and my dad were at Saint Mary's on that teaching thing—I think we even have this book—

JASON: Yeah. Your dad. Knows everyone. Whatever. I bought this for you because it's my favorite. (Right now. Right now it's my favorite.) So, say thank you, okay? *Comprende?* Learn to take a gift. Say fucking thank you.

ABBY: Thank you.

(ABBY and JASON share a moment—)

JASON: "the stalks are very prickly, a penalty they earn for knowing the black art of blackberry-making..." —Galway Kinnell

See, that's you. The prickly part. Anyway, forget it. You already have it or something.

ABBY: No. I mean, I haven't read it. I just, know him.

JASON: You should read it.

ABBY: I will.

JASON: You don't know everything.

ABBY: I know.

JASON: You might be pretty and you might be bold, but you don't know everything.

## a couple of nice times

CLEA: You were with him how long?

ABBY: A couple months. Five or six.

CLEA: And then you broke up with him.

ABBY: I wanted to date someone else. The Spanish guy. In Spain. Jason sort of freaked out when my dad and I came back from Spain. He stopped working for us. He went away.

CLEA: Completely?

ABBY: Well. Every now and then he'd send some weird inappropriate letter. I didn't answer them. Mostly.

CLEA: Hmmm...

ABBY: There were a couple of nice times. Like one night I went up to his place, way the fuck uptown. We just, like, made dinner. But it was so nice. Just making dinner. And then we went up to the roof and he told me about being 16. How he took this trip to the Grand Canyon with his older brother and they smeared mud all over their faces. He called me a wise child.

CLEA: Wise child?

ABBY: Salinger.

CLEA: Oh. He should have written about that.

ABBY: Instead, there is this—

CLEA: Work of problematic angst featuring you.


### jameson addie

(ABBY, *as in* JASON's *book*— *A deadly dirty little girl.*)

ABBY: In the book, in Jason's book, my name is Jameson Addie. I'm a New York City girl, and Jason, whose name is Wolf (HIS NAME IS WOLF!!??), fucks me again and again on my dad's black leather chair. This really happened in real life, it's where I lost it, you know, but in the book it seems to happen again and again and again and in the book, there is this event, totally blown out of proportion where I won't give him a blowjob. One night. Once. O-N-C-E.

Wolf says, You're a good girl, and when he says it, I feel like cream, sweet cream, buttermilk and Iowa pie. Cherry pie. From Iowa.

Wolf can't feel anything. He says it a lot. So I hurt him. To make him feel.

Anyway. I'm just using Wolf 'til I get into Harvard. My dad went there. My dad teaches there too. Have you read my dad's new book? My dad is the best writer in the whole world. Wolf is an idiot. He'll never be my dad. But he'll make my dad a hero. And then everyone will break everyone's heart. It all just can't be helped.

## plans begin to form. impulsive plans.

ABBY: I'm going there.

(JAMES *appears.*)

JAMES: Where?

ABBY: London.

JAMES: Why would you possibly want to do that?

ABBY: To tell him off.

JAMES: Darling, can't you call instead?

ABBY: I think I should go.

JAMES: This would be a bad idea.

ABBY: We need to talk.

JAMES: And so you're going to cross the ocean?

ABBY: Yes. We need to talk face to face. He wrote about me. He wrote mean, untrue things.

JAMES: Darling Daughter—

ABBY: He called and begged me to go there. And I think it's the best way to work things out with the most compassion and equanimity.

(JAMES *might snort here.*)

JAMES: Writers say a lot of things. I wouldn't take any of it seriously. I have said a great many things to a great many women—

ABBY: He's not you.

JAMES: That's evident. I have talent.

ABBY: I'm going.

JAMES: You're paying for it on your own.

ABBY: I have savings. I have frequent flyer miles.

JAMES: Good.

ABBY: Good.

(CLEA *appears.*)

CLEA: I'm coming with you.

ABBY: Really? You'd really come?

CLEA: Of course. You shouldn't be alone when you kill him. When you rip his heart out.

ABBY: His heart, and then his hands. I will rip them out of the wrist sockets. He will never write again.

CLEA: This is so Titus.

ABBY: Fuck Titus.

CLEA: Oh, no. Voice activated software...

ABBY: What about it?

CLEA: Well, I'm just saying, there is voice activated software. So he can still—

ABBY: Who's side are you on?

CLEA: Yours.

ABBY: I will rip Jason's hands off with my teeth and tear out his vocal cords and poison his imagination, his mind, his craft. I will poison him against writing. Murderous Everything.

CLEA: We can get cheap tickets on the web.

ABBY: I have frequent flyer miles. And we'll stay with him. After we inflict injury and get revenge. I mean, I'm sure we could stay with him.

CLEA: Interesting paradox. But I'm sure you know what you're doing.

ABBY: Fuck the eternal now. This is war.

CLEA: We're going to London.

## scrambling

CLEA: We scramble. I cash in my paycheck from the work study job and I am able to get this really cheap ticket on the web. I am able to get a passport in a one day emergency rush. I've never had one before. Abby already has a passport, but she goes with me to the passport office, just because this is what friends do. I go to London to help me her inflict torture and she goes to the passport office to save me from frustration with bureaucratic waiting. She is my best friend who I adore more than anyone in the world even more than my idol the superstar celebrity pregnant icon, who is also in London. And two days later, we are on a plane to the United Kingdom. London, England. Heathrow Airport. Virgin Atlantic. Reading Jason's book. Again.

*(Girls on plane;* JASON's *lines may be staged with the actor physically in the scene or with voice-overs.)*

JASON: ...a dirty little blonde, an unfeeling bone-colored bitch, her fingers twirling her hair in a diner on Sixth Avenue, while I ate shit and drank coffee...

ABBY: He's so dramatic.

CLEA: I'm kind of getting sick of hearing what a dirty little girl you were. Does he have to keep saying it over and over again?

ABBY: It's repetition.

CLEA: Yeah.

ABBY: No, I mean, he's doing it on purpose. It's a technique. He's a Gertrude Stein person.

CLEA: Well, it bugs (me).

JASON: "...you fade me out, turn to ice, stop wanting me, how can you stop wanting me when I could just stay with my legs wrapped around yours for hours and hours? but you withdraw, change your mind and tell your friends, and I see you all together, giggling like you know something you don't—and I want to fuck them to get you back, but it doesn't even matter, because I win. Don't you get it? I have the final word. "

(*Pause.* ABBY *and* CLEA *are horrified.*)

CLEA: Why is he holding on to this thing with you?

ABBY: Writers hold on to things.

CLEA: I don't.

ABBY: You're not a writer.

CLEA: But if I were...I'm just saying, this book disturbs me.

ABBY: Art is disturbing.

CLEA: I don't think it's art. Do you think it's art?

ABBY: Don't try to make me feel better. Watch the cheerleader movie.

(ABBY *goes back to the book.* CLEA *doesn't watch the movie.*)

### arrival

ABBY: (*Affecting a formal voice, as if in a guidebook*) Declare yourself a tourist.

CLEA: (*In her own voice*) Just to be here is beautiful. Thrilling and strange.

ABBY: Exchange your dollars for pounds.

CLEA: I am shocked to find our American money doesn't go very far. It's roughly half of what it'd be worth at home.

ABBY: Become accustomed to feeling like an American. Less than refined.

CLEA: Shit. It's expensive here. I'm glad we'll be staying with Jason. That's all I can say.

(ABBY *drops her guidebook tone.*)

ABBY: The exchange rate sucks. But, it'll be fine. Jason'll take us out, pay for us. I'm his muse. He owes us.

CLEA: Good. 'Cause I'm gonna be broke by lunch tomorrow.

ABBY: Too bad you have to eat. That's what makes it expensive. All that eating.

CLEA: Normal people eat.

ABBY: I'm just saying it's expensive.

CLEA: Are you gonna call him?

ABBY: Oh. Right. You need a telephone card in Britain. Maybe we should just show up.

CLEA: What time did you say we were coming?

ABBY: Lets just show up.

CLEA: Do you know how to, where he lives?

ABBY: Sure. We can take the Tube.

CLEA: This is going to be fantastic. Smashing.

(*Disparate elements come together in an overlapped fusion soundscape—Madonna music, British Punk, Indian raga, text from Jason's book are sampled and mixed. The expectation of London and all that the girls believe this trip will hold.*)

(ABBY *and* CLEA *"arrive".*)

(*Lights down*)

## END OF ACT ONE

# ACT TWO

*(Sound cue as the act begins:)*

JASON: *(V O)* You've reached the prerecorded Jason Stark. I'm away 'til the 4th, leave a message, or if it's urgent, you can call my agent... Have you read my book? Have you read my book about Abby Meadow? My book, my book, my book, my book...dirty little blonde my book.... I'm totally unreachable.

*(Lights up.* ABBY *and* CLEA *and their backpacks.)*

CLEA: He didn't know we were coming?

ABBY: Well.

CLEA: Well, what?

ABBY: I mean, I know he lives here. He called me. He asked me to come.

CLEA: And did you tell him you were?

ABBY: Well.

CLEA: Well, what?

ABBY: I thought we could surprise him. In all the scrambling and whatever, I just—

CLEA: You didn't tell him.

ABBY: Well.

CLEA: You've got to stop saying that.

ABBY: Okay, look. He'll be back soon. We'll go to a hostel. We'll leave messages. And in the meantime, we will get our bearings. We will see London and get acclimated here. Do you have, can I look at...the *Lonely Planet* guide?

(CLEA *has a copy of* Lonely Planet London, *which* ABBY *takes from her.*)

CLEA: It is a lonely planet isn't it? It shouldn't be. But sometimes it is.

ABBY: Don't be dramatic. I'm glad you brought this.

CLEA: I was hoping it'd say something about where Madonna's living, you know, because I figured after we cut Jason's balls off, I might need something to do. I hope getting acclimated doesn't cost much.

ABBY: Okay. Something close.

CLEA: And cheap.

ABBY: Easy.

### the palace hotel, a nice little place

NICKY: Welcome to the Palace Hotel. A nice little place in Bayswater. It's not much, but it's ours. Girls on this side. Blokes on the other. It's fourteen pounds a night, please pay in advance for the night you'll be staying. There's tea in the tea room, and it's free, though you should bring your own mug, messages are over here, there's email on two computers, five pounds for twenty minutes, and you have to sign the guest register. Please sign the guest register. Where are you from?

CLEA: New York.

NICKY: Very good. I want to go to New York.

ABBY: Of course you do.

NICKY: I'm a musician.

ABBY: Of course you are.

CLEA: Excuse her, she's very tired. I'm Clea. Do you know where Madonna lives?

ABBY: Oh, God.

NICKY: We call her Madge over here. She's pregnant, you know.

CLEA: I know. I know everything about her. Except her address in London. Do you know where she does yoga?

ABBY: Can we go to our room?

NICKY: Sure. Upstairs on the left. The key's in the door. You're sharing with a couple of Swedish girls. They're very nice. And you pay each morning for that night. Did I already say that?

(ABBY *and* CLEA *nod.*)

NICKY: Right. Do you know yet, the tenure of your—

ABBY: A few days. (*To* CLEA) You coming?

CLEA: Sure. (*To* NICKY, *in a dramatic whisper*) Do you think later we could conference on The Whereabouts?

ABBY: Come on.

NICKY: Good night.

(*He is already slightly mesmerized by funny little* CLEA.)

## clea can't sleep

(CLEA *sits at the lobby desk where* NICKY *works. She can't sleep.*)

CLEA: She makes it okay for a girl to be ambitious. To want. She takes things we think of as "bad"—ambition, sex, Catholicism—and reinvents them so that—

NICKY: Look. She's got no talent. I'm a musician. I don't mean to knock your idol or anything but, I'm a musician. And her—

CLEA: NO TALENT? How can you say no talent!? I'm going to pretend you didn't say that. What about postmodernism and appropriation? Gender iconography in the late twentieth century? She didn't just do yoga. She did Kabbalah. She did burning crosses. She Vogued.

NICKY: She did Vogue.

CLEA: Yes. And she did Evita. The Argentines freaked, but controversy feeds her whole deal.

NICKY: Okay, but Evita, besides being the wife of a very disturbing dictator—

CLEA: (*Cutting him off*) The tabloids say, Madonna: Has She Gone Too Far?

But I say, Is there such a thing? Is there such a thing when you are Madonna and the world is your oyster because you never let anyone tell you who to be or what to do or what your limitations are? No. No. There is no such thing. Get into the groove. Open your heart. Express yourself, don't repress yourself. Music makes the people come together. The Bourgeoisie and the Rebel.

NICKY: Does she really say "bourgeoisie"?

CLEA: Yes. We have a lot in common. Her and me, not you and me though maybe you and me have a lot in common too, I don't know yet, but her and me, she and I, we have a bond. We're both from Detroit. And that's not all. The list goes on and on.

NICKY: D-Town!

CLEA: Mo Town.

NICKY: The Def Jam of another era.

CLEA: Loads of very creative people come from Detroit. Like Madonna and Diana Ross and me. And cars are made there. So you see. We are deeply connected by our Root Geography. And, okay this sounds fantastic but it's true—we were tigers in another life and she scratched my eyes out. It's okay though.

NICKY: Did you say you can't sleep?

CLEA: Yes.

NICKY: It's common. Your first night somewhere new.

CLEA: You think?

NICKY: Oh yes. Very common.

CLEA: This is my first time out of the country.

NICKY: I see.

CLEA: Except Canada. From Detroit, you can just drive into Canada.

NICKY: Well, then it's very common. To not sleep.

CLEA: Thank you.

NICKY: I'm here all night. Watching the desk. So you can talk to me.

CLEA: Night shift?

NICKY: Right.

CLEA: I understand. I work in Admissions.

NICKY: Right. Well, so you can stay, if you want.

CLEA: Thanks.

NICKY: Not at all. (*Beat*) Will you see the sights while you're in London? There are great sights.

CLEA: We're kind of here on business.

NICKY: I see.

CLEA: Yes. There may not be time for sights.

NICKY: What kind of business?

CLEA: Well, waiting for Her to give birth. But also, see, I'm actually her illegitimate secret daughter from the early days in Detroit and I need to let her know that I exist, which I plan to do when I find her in downward facing dog at the yoga center. Or at her house, when I slip a note with my half of the secret locket, the one my adopted mom gave me when I turned eighteen, to her doorman.

No, I'm totally lying. Really, really what happened is: *(In one big gulp)* Jason Stark, he's this writer Abby lost her virginity with when she was sixteen, he wrote a book about her and called her in the middle of the night to let her know that the book has come out and it's like, essentially all about how much she sucked as a person, but how he wants her anyway, and he needs her to be with him because he's losing his mind or something, and I'm here because I am her best friend. But Abby was retarded and didn't tell Jason we were coming so we got here and he was, I don't even know where he is, but I don't have any money, I mean, I have like ten pounds or something for the whole weekend, after paying for this place. So, he has to show up soon so I can eat. Abby doesn't eat, but I like need to.

NICKY: I have food. If you run out of money. I have just, you know, you can come to me. I'm staff. I will feed you.

CLEA: That's very nice.

NICKY: Oh. Don't mention it. I'm staff.

CLEA: I wish I were more like her.

NICKY: Madonna? Or your friend?

CLEA: Both. They're very fierce. You know, both their moms died when they were little. Why can't one of my stupid parents be dead? I mean, I don't really want them to be dead, but it's so much more romantic than working for Chrysler, you know? How about you? Are your parents dead?

NICKY: No. They're quite alive. On British soil.

CLEA: See what I mean? Do you collect things?

NICKY: I do.

CLEA: I thought so. What do you collect?

NICKY: Guitar strings. Picks. Music magazines. Gabardine shirts. You?

CLEA: Bracelets. And gloves, not the keep-warm kind, but the old lady lace kind.

NICKY: Candy wrappers.

CLEA: Sure.

NICKY: It's a weird one.

CLEA: No, I get it.

NICKY: I just like the way they look.

CLEA: I know. I went through a gum wrapper phase myself. The colors...

NICKY: Right.

CLEA: I love the colors.

NICKY: The green ones.

CLEA: Right.


## clea worries, abby frets

CLEA: Why aren't there any vegetarians in England?

ABBY: There's a lot of butter.

CLEA: What do I eat here?

ABBY: Scones. And lots of butter. If you can take butter.

CLEA: I need vegetables.

ABBY: Can't help ya. This is England. Scones and lots of butter.

CLEA: Someone at the hostel last night called America "the Evil Empire". She was wearing Nike's.

ABBY: The Brits used to own India. Everyone's been the Evil Empire some time or other.

CLEA: She wasn't British. I think she was German or something.

ABBY: Exactly.

CLEA: I had insomnia.

ABBY: I thought you were so tired...

CLEA: I was. But in the room with the Swedish girls, I had insomnia. I stayed up talking to—

ABBY: We'll go to Jason's house. It'll all work out. He just...

CLEA: Isn't here.

ABBY: Right.

CLEA: Maybe we need a plan. I'm going to run out of money.

ABBY: We'll hear from him.

CLEA: We have to. Cause I'm gonna run out of money.

ABBY: He worships me.

CLEA: Well, that's good. 'Cause I'm gonna run out of money.

## hard at work

(JASON *now affects a fake British accent.*)

JASON: The young writer Jason Stark smokes too many cigarettes and drinks whiskey. He is hot on the trail of his new book. He has gone away, left the city impulsively. Locked himself in a small hotel room in a small town with a bottle of whiskey and the desire to write. And occasionally girls he brings home from the local pub. The waitresses there are something to behold.

A new book. A new heroine. Her name is Roxanne. No, her name is Nicolette. No, it's Roxanne. And she's smashing. Positively smashing. Young and slightly naughty. Roxanne, Roxanne, I want to be your man.

Oh. No.

(*He hurls something across the room. Then he tries again.*)

Her name is Gabby. Short for Gabrielle. She's mute. Born that way. She gives...Ax...the hero...no, maybe his name is...Rex...she gives him a blowjob in the opening scene, and he thinks this is like the best thing ever because he's never gotten a blowjob before from a girl who can't talk. It's pretty wild. A turn-on. It lasts for *hours*. And her dad, he's this famous... painter. Like Picasso. And he paints his mute daughter a lot. Until she runs away with Rex/Ax and they live in a ... well, it's like a shack cause he's really poor and they're like, like the road warriors in *Road Warrior*, it's futuristic, and...

Well. At least we know there is Gabby and Rex.

And Rox. Roxanne. Roxanne, who I have to call. She gets really mad if I keep her waiting. Roxanne, little slut pub waitress with electric hair, messy and flying about her face. I love it.

### a real writer

JAMES: I wrote a story about Abby once. It was soon
after her mother died. Abby asked where her mother
had gone, and I wrote to answer. There was another
story, incidental, and a scene in the Eden Trilogy that
came the day my best friend noticed that my daughter
had breasts. Which was awful, if you ask me. Just
awful. And I guess one might say that Constance,
the sister of the narrator in *Grass in the Blade* sounds
something like Abby. I might have used some of her
syntax, although probably without noticing it much.
But the point is, a Real Writer will transmute the source
material. Not so much disguise it as let it all digest and
settle in the unconscious, so that later, you see there
is a marriage between the real and the imagined. It
all pours out in an undistinguishable reshaped new
form. Of course, the problem is that everything in the
writer's domain is up for grabs. It becomes material.
Who is to say what and who are drawn from... what
and whom.

### green park with swans the size of buicks

ABBY: I found him.

CLEA: Guy Ritchie?

ABBY: Jason.

CLEA: Oh. Right.

ABBY: He's giving a reading the day after tomorrow.
Some bookstore. West End. We're going to be there.

CLEA: *(Referring to* NICKY*)* All of us?

ABBY: *(Getting it)* I guess.

CLEA: You are still killing him, aren't you?

ABBY: Of course.

CLEA: Because we did not come all this way for any lesser action.

ABBY: Trust me. I'll poison him against writing. Which is the same as killing. It's more deadly than killing.

CLEA: So long as we take revenge. Or avenge. Are we avenging or revenging?

ABBY: We're revenging.

CLEA: Because I am worried that the focus is shifting from "killing" to "shocking."

ABBY: I think you should fake a seizure.

CLEA: Excuse me?

ABBY: At the reading. I'll be sitting next to you, and then, when they have to stop the reading and carry you off, he'll see me, and I'll stand. But, first, you convulse.

CLEA: Can't we confront him directly?

NICKY: They do say that direct methods—

ABBY: I just think convulsions will be interesting.

CLEA: Well. Sure. But I'm kind of a direct girl myself. I don't know if I can be convincing convulsing.

NICKY: Uh, hate to interupt, but uh, I rather agree with— (*Motioning towards* CLEA)

ABBY: I'm sorry. Who are you again?

CLEA: Remember? He's Nicky. From the hostel.

NICKY: Well, not really *from* the hostel. Originally North London. At the Palace about two years. The *hotel*, not the, well, not the actual "*palace*". And I'm a musician, classical violin ten years, then I began to experiment with emergent forms, abstract and then street influenced, I listened to quite a bit of strange French pop music, but then New York started calling, as they say, since, well, there's really a fusion there of street and also—

ABBY: Okay. I get it. I thought you were just some guy who worked at the hostel.

CLEA: Nicky is a stellar being.

ABBY: Great. Because I thought he was just some guy who worked at the hostel.

CLEA: Excuse her. She's very tired.

ABBY: Okay. So long as I know who—

CLEA: What about Madonna's House? Can we—? The Swedish girls said—

ABBY: I doubt the Swedish girls would know.

CLEA: She said, "I'm having a love affair with England." I want to have a love affair with England.

NICKY: Right.

ABBY: Please stop talking about her. We have to focus on Jason right now.

CLEA: Abby is in a very bad mood.

ABBY: Abby is in a fine mood. Clea has some strange attachment to celebrity street maps.

CLEA: They're called Star Maps.
Look. I am financially challenged and single minded. There is one thing I want to do in this country, just one. I don't like butter. I just want this one thing. Can't we just do this one thing that I want to do!?

ABBY: There will be plenty of time later for Madonna sightings. Right now, we have to have priorities. Which means you have to convulse.

CLEA: I'm here to have a love affair with England!

NICKY: I could show you Princess Diana's House.

ABBY: Oh, no, not Princess Diana's House.

CLEA: *(To* NICKY*)* We're sorry she's dead, but we don't want to go there. *(To* ABBY*)* But what about, I mean, you know who I mean. With Child and Empire?

NICKY: The Queen?

ABBY: Clea. This is called stalking, and famous people don't like it. She is not some icon for your consumption, she's a person. Probably not even very nice.

NICKY: I'm sure the house is fairly hidden and—

ABBY: You need a role model. And I don't think she's the right one.

CLEA: You're just never had anything like this. A person you believed in—

ABBY: When I was in India, I met people with gurus.

CLEA: Sure.

NICKY: My aunt, she follows that woman with the peacock feather—

ABBY: But Madonna is not an enlightened being.

CLEA: How do you know?

NICKY: I do sort of doubt she's enlightened. That takes a lot of work, doesn't it? I mean, her mixes are all right, but "enlightened" conjures up images of—

ABBY: She's a pop star. Not even rock.

CLEA: So? Nobody said "That Joan of Arc, she isn't a saint, just a soldier. Not even a soldier. Just a girl with a..." what did they have then? Spears? Lancets? What did they have?

NICKY: I think they had swords.

CLEA: Right.

ABBY: They did so say that! Anyway, it doesn't matter.

CLEA: It did to them.

ABBY: What I'm getting at is—

CLEA: I know what you're getting at.

ABBY: It's just like Jason. Don't you see that?

NICKY: Jason's the one with the "dirty little girl" book?

CLEA: No. It's not like that at all.

ABBY: Fine.

CLEA: It's not.

ABBY: Sure.

CLEA: I didn't fuck her and write a book about it.

NICKY: Oh, right. Jason is the bloke with the—

ABBY: It's the waiting period. I'm going to go completely crazy if I have to wait much longer. I'm not good at waiting. Why wasn't he here?

CLEA: You didn't call first.

ABBY: Why is there this waiting period?

CLEA: You didn't call.

ABBY: No. It's not that. We're just waiting. That's all we do. And we can't spend money because Somebody is financially challenged.

NICKY: Lots of things are free.

CLEA: It's "The Eternal Now".

(ABBY *scowls*.)

NICKY: (*Breaking up the fight*) Okay. Time to see sights. We will go to the museums. The Tate's free, and I'll pay the Tube fare. Come on. Both of you.

| ABBY: | CLEA: |
|-------|-------|
| No.   | Yes.  |

CLEA: Well?

NICKY: I'll wait over there. By the big swans.

ABBY: You go. I have stuff to do.

CLEA: Come with us. Please?

ABBY: I'll find you later.

CLEA: Are you sure?

ABBY: Sure.

CLEA: I— (*As if to say I'm sorry/I love you...*)

ABBY: Really. It's fine.

(CLEA *leaves.*)

(ABBY *takes out* JASON'*s book. Begins to read again. She strikes the pose of Jameson Addie.*)

### outside the tate modern, which is free

(NICKY *is attempting to draw* CLEA *who keeps inadvertently moving.*)

CLEA: She's different. I mean, this is not the strong willed exuberant fuck you Abby of our youth. Mine and hers, not mine and yours.

NICKY: She's upset.

CLEA: Abby?

NICKY: Under pressure. Hold still.

CLEA: Abby doesn't get upset. She doesn't eat, remember?

NICKY: Hold—

CLEA: I know, still. I've never been drawn before. And I think that was our first fight. Mine and hers, not mine and yours.

NICKY: Yes, I know. Keep your head still.

CLEA: Sorry.

NICKY: It takes twenty drawings to know a face.

CLEA: It's thrilling. To be drawn. Does that mean we have nineteen more?

NICKY: You've got to stop moving, Cle.

CLEA: I know. Sorry. Do you think it's me? Or do you think she's different too?

NICKY: This is where you really have got to stop moving altogether.

CLEA: It's terrible having to sit still. I might not be able to stand nineteen more.

NICKY: Come on. Just...breathe.

(CLEA *breathes*.)

NICKY: Without moving. Breathe without moving.

(CLEA *tries to do this*.)

CLEA: Can I draw you back?

NICKY: In a minute.

CLEA: Nobody told me this would be work.

(*Beat*)

NICKY: There. I'm done. We can switch.

(CLEA *and* NICKY *switch roles. He hands her the pad and pencils*.)

CLEA: Ah. Much better.

(CLEA *moves now, delighting in doing so. She positions* NICKY *for her drawing. Moving all the time*)

NICKY: Do you draw?

CLEA: I do now.

### so at home

JASON: No, I'm not British. I'm sensitive to sound.
I'm an artist. I absorb. In the States, I was always an
outsider. But here I feel I belong. So, I can't help it,
Roxanne, if I speak this way. I feel at home here. Your
people are mine. Your sounds and inflections. I've
never felt so at home.

### an easy target

ABBY: She wasn't a dirty little girl. She was smart and
lonely. And you're right, Jason. An easy target. Just
waiting to be found.

### a boy in a post feeling age

JASON: We are in a post feeling age. Nobody in *The New
York Times* Sunday magazine or book review can feel.
Indie film doesn't feel. The Face doesn't feel. Interview
never felt. It has all been taken from us. Where do you
think our feelings have gone, Roxanne? Do you know?
Do you care? Do you want to hear about my book?

### like a little prayer

CLEA: In this moment, I feel we need to acknowledge
that Jason Stark is wrong. It is not an unfeeling age, not
an age of dead vacant people. It's just not. Because I'm
here, and I feel and I want and I'm good. And Abby's
here. And Nicky's here. And I could just not know
this person, Nicky, and come to England and here he
is, just waiting for me to show up and rock his world.
Who could have known? I mean, who could have
known?

## where the goddess lives, waiting

NICKY: I found out where she lives.

CLEA: I love you.

NICKY: The general area. Yeah?

CLEA: For finding her house. The general area.

NICKY: Oh. Right. Well. We'll go there. Tonight.

CLEA: You're going to take me?

NICKY: Can't have you getting lost on your pilgrimage. Pilgrims usually have a guide.

CLEA: She's going to have her baby soon. And her new C D will be released. The cycle of creation goes around and around.

(NICKY *impulsively kisses* CLEA.)

NICKY: I've been wanting to do that all weekend. Is it okay?

(CLEA *nods. Speechless and delighted*)

CLEA: Can I do it back?

(NICKY *nods.* CLEA *kisses him back. It's fabulous.*)

## chapter 86. last paragraph, cherry pie

JASON: Once upon a time, there was an ugly ducking. A misfit boy who traveled to New York City where, by virtue of his talent, drive and hunger, and one devastating love affair, he became a handsome prince. I want you to see me like this, Jameson, Jameson Addie, inane carcass, lethal intoxicant, girl. I want you to see me handsome. And a prince. Because I still hate everything in the world except the way I felt with you.

## hating everything: abby and jason, five years ago

ABBY: That's pretty strong.

JASON: I guess.

ABBY: Why do you hate everything?

JASON: Don't you?

ABBY: I don't know. I don't think I hate everything. No.

JASON: What do you not hate?

ABBY: Being alive. I don't hate being alive. My friends.
My dad. Travel. Poetry. The way the stars look at
night, especially when you're out of the City. Lots of
things. There are lots of things I do not hate.

JASON: I wish I were like you. You're a very wise child.

ABBY: I'm not a child.

JASON: It was a literary reference. Salinger.

ABBY: Fucking writers.

JASON: What?

ABBY: Nothing. I just hate fucking writers and their
fucking literary fucking references.

JASON: I want to stay like this, with you, forever.

ABBY: No, you don't. You'll have stuff you want to do.

JASON: No. Nothing.

ABBY: Um, how about graduate and get your M F A?
Write a book. You'll want to do that. And even on a
very basic level, you'll want to get up from here so you
can do basic things. Like shave or whatever.

JASON: No. I'll grow a beard. A long one. I'll stop
eating. I can write a book from here, from the roof, in
the middle of this one night with you.

ABBY: Well, I'm going to want to do stuff. I don't want
to stay here forever.

JASON: Sure you do. You want to stay with me. Forever. Who else will adore you like this?

ABBY: Someone will.

JASON: No. Never. No one will ever love you like me. And I will love you forever. Just like this.

### meanwhile...

(ABBY *prepares for the reading.*)

CLEA: You look great.

ABBY: I look old.

CLEA: You can't look old. We're twenty-one.

ABBY: I look fat.

CLEA: You can't look fat. You don't eat.

ABBY: He liked me when I was sixteen and going to Spence. Now I'm aging and fat.

CLEA: You're not aging and you're not fat. I like it here.

ABBY: It's okay.

CLEA: Have you ever been drawn?

ABBY: Sure.

CLEA: He got that thing I do with my mouth.

ABBY: What are you talking about?

(CLEA *does the thing.*)

ABBY: Oh, that.

CLEA: I get why she likes it here.

ABBY: She likes it because she's in love. People do all kind of things out of the mythology of romantic love.

CLEA: Yes. They do.

ABBY: Do I look okay?

CLEA: You look beautiful. *(Beat)* You'll kick ass. You'll kick his ass, but also, you'll kick ass.

ABBY: Right. I will kick ass.

## the reading

*(Enter* JASON. *Steps up to a podium, about to start his reading, takes a sip from a glass of water)*

*(*ABBY *and* CLEA *are unseen.)*

*(*JASON *experiences all sorts of technical difficulties, the mike is weird, something in the air feels wrong. He finds himself unusually tongue-tied as The Young Writer Jason Stark and the skinny kid from Iowa tango in his mind.)*

JASON: Hello. I'm Jason Stark.

*(Some applause.* NICKY *and* CLEA *attempt to hijack through loud coughs, noises, throat-clearing, the dropping of objects, etc....)*

JASON: Thank you. This is my first novel... It's set in....

CLEA: *(Heckling)* I'm not in a post feeling age. My feelings are fine.

NICKY: Mine are all right.

*(*ABBY *hushes them more aggressively.)*

JASON: Well, see there was a girl...sixteen, smashing and mean...see, first there was this Smiths song, it was before her time...but when I said... "sixteen, smashing, and..." I was referring to the cadence of...

*(*NICKY *and* CLEA *attempt to make more noise.* ABBY *hushes them.)*

JASON: ...and then, blackberries...well I liked that poem and the power of making language, the black art of making...well, fruit of course....

(JASON *sees* ABBY *out of the very corners of his eye—or mind's eye, or memory—he isn't even sure. She still affects him that way—a mixture of dread and desire, attraction and fear—it's hot. But freaky.*)

JASON: She seduced me! I did not seduce her. She started it. She kissed me first, told me I was stupid! Oh, she was mean, she was mean...she kissed me first but would never give me a blowjob, and I'm sure she had done it before, this guy she was with before me, he was like...she was beautiful, my God, she was beautiful, and self assured...I wish I could be her, only I couldn't be her, that would be weird, but she was my ideal. Perfect. And— (*He realizes that yes indeed, she really is there, right where he thinks she is.*) —Here. She is here. Why is she here?

(ABBY *stands. They face one another.*)

ABBY: Hi, Jason.

(*Blackout*)

### (another) surprise!

(*Lights up*)

ABBY: This is Clea, and her friend.

NICKY: Nicky. Pleased to—

CLEA: We hate your book.

JASON: Thanks.

ABBY: Clea has to go now.

CLEA: I'm on a pilgrimage.

JASON: Really?

ABBY: So, bye.

(CLEA *leaves while silently gesturing secret things to* ABBY *about killing* JASON *but having mercy while she does this.*)

(ABBY *and* JASON *are now alone.*)

ABBY: She's protective.

JASON: What are you doing here?

ABBY: I came to see you. You begged, remember?

JASON: But I didn't think you'd really come.

ABBY: So buy me a drink.

JASON: I can't believe you're here.

ABBY: You begged.

JASON: But you really came. It's so rash.

ABBY: Yeah.

JASON: Indeed.

ABBY: You said you needed me to write.

JASON: You said to go fuck someone else.

ABBY: You said I was your muse.

JASON: Well. You were. You were my muse.

ABBY: So I'm here.

JASON: But I did it.

ABBY: You did what?

JASON: What you said.

ABBY: What did I say?

JASON: I fucked someone else.

ABBY: Oh.

JASON: And wrote about it. The writing's not that great, actually, but it gave me hope.

ABBY: I see.

JASON: Can I take you to dinner or something?

ABBY: Dinner? Can you take me to dinner? You can fucking pay my bills for the last three days is what you can do. Fuck! Fucking self centered, narcissistic, writers who cannibalize other people for their—

JASON: Do you think you're just mad at your father?

ABBY: Okay, that's really it. YOU CALLED ME. I AM YOUR MUSE. DO YOU NOT REMEMBER THIS PART? YOU CALLED ME.

JASON: Come on. Let me take you to dinner.

ABBY: Dinner is the least you can take me to. Asshole.

### never forget who you are

CLEA: You're a ray of light. A superstar. A lucky star. You get up again, over and over. Don't let them tell you you're nothing. They'll try. Over and over. They will tell you to be small. And you will say, No. They will tell you to go away. And you will not go away. They will tell you to stop, and you will say "Don't tell me to stop." You can be loud, vulgar and overly publicized. But you're here. And so am I.

### at the house of her holiness

(NICKY *and* CLEA *outside Madonna's house. They are quiet.*)

NICKY: This is it. It's through that fence over there. It's hard to see.

CLEA: I can't believe you found it.

NICKY: Oh. It was nothing. Well, I mean I had to do research and bribe that girl from, but it was—

CLEA: (*Reverent*) We should be quiet.

NICKY: You think?

CLEA: Sure.

*(Beat)*

*(*CLEA *and* NICKY *are quiet. They wait. Reverently. They kiss.)*

CLEA: Do you think we'll know each other?

NICKY: Us? Or you and Madonna?

CLEA: Us.

NICKY: Yes. I think we will know each other.

CLEA: Do you think we can be new?

NICKY: New how?

CLEA: New in all ways. In every moment. *(Beat)* Want to go?

NICKY: This is important to you.

CLEA: I think Abby's right.

NICKY: No. It's important to you. Lets wait.

*(Beat)*

CLEA: You're nice.

NICKY: Oh. No. It's fine.

CLEA: Do you want to go?

NICKY: I told you, I really don't mind.

CLEA: I know. It's just... Do you know what I mean?

NICKY: Well...

CLEA: She's still my hero.

NICKY: Of course.

CLEA: It's just right now I'd rather be with you.

NICKY: Then...

CLEA: Lets go.

### drunk on chardonnay and love—

JASON: You're amazing.

ABBY: I thought you were with someone else.

JASON: I was. But I was lying to myself. Roxanne was nothing.

ABBY: Roxanne? Was that her name?

JASON: It's amazing. You. You're still amazing.

ABBY: You were right. I do think about you.

JASON: You were right too.

ABBY: What was I right about? Fucking Roxanne?

JASON: You were right about everything.

ABBY: Here we are in London. You wrote that disgusting book. And here we are.

JASON: It isn't disgusting.

ABBY: It is. Do you know what you did to me?

JASON: I lay a garland of roses at your feet.

ABBY: Fuck that. You made me an oversexed, mean-spirited freak. What the Hell is a dirty little girl anyway? I mean, it's fucked up how you just—

JASON: It's not fucked up. I immortalized you, I said no one would ever love you like me, and I was right. Lets go back to my place.

ABBY: Okay.

### everyone at everyone else's place

(NICKY *takes* CLEA *to his room at the hostel. Somewhat awkwardly at first, they kiss. This blossoms into a fabulous, and slightly awkward, make out session.*)

(*Meanwhile, on the other side of the city* ABBY *and* JASON *violently bust through the door, hit the walls and sink to the floor making love.*)

(*Blackout on both couples*)

### lost to us all

(CLEA *waits for* ABBY, *bags at her feet.*)

CLEA: In the early hours of the morning Madonna gave birth to a boy. It was a C Section. She was rushed to the hospital, and if I had stayed in my hiding place all night, I might have seen her as she emerged from the house and into the waiting automobile which whisked her into the dawn. However, I was busy. With Nicky. And now it's time. Our flight leaves in a few hours. There's just Abby. Who isn't here. Apparantly there were two empty beds in the room with the Swedish Girls.

(ABBY *appears, coat on, no suitcase.*)

CLEA: Where have you been!?

ABBY: I was with Jason.

CLEA: Jason!? Whoa. That's—okay, story on plane. We have to get to the airport. If you're not there a whole hour and a half in advance, they do not let you on the plane. I was informed about this last night—

ABBY: I'm staying.

CLEA: No. You're coming home with me. Come on.

ABBY: No. I'm staying with Jason. He doesn't know yet. It's a surprise.

CLEA: You can't. Jason's horrible.

ABBY: He's fragile.

CLEA: He's horrible.

ABBY: Not inside.

CLEA: Abby. You cannot stay here. What about college? What about the Buddha?

ABBY: Jason and I love each other.

CLEA: You and Jason do not love each other. Go get your suitcase.

ABBY: You're jealous. It's totally understandable, Cle. You don't have anyone of your own, and it's time to outgrow your movie star fixations, but you haven't found an acceptable substitute—

CLEA: That's wrong.

ABBY: You need to have a lot of sex.

CLEA: How do you know I'm not having a lot of sex?

ABBY: Are you having sex?

CLEA: Maybe.

ABBY: Who are you...? Oh, Front Desk ? You two hooked up?

CLEA: No time for this. Get your stuff. Now.

ABBY: Listen I know this is hard for you to understand, but I can't go anywhere right now. Jason needs me. He's like my dad.

CLEA: You hate your dad.

ABBY: I don't hate my dad.

CLEA: Yes, you do. Everyone knows you hate your dad.

ABBY: Who is everyone?

CLEA: Everyone that we know together knows that you hate your dad. This is very available knowledge.

ABBY: My dad—

CLEA: —Is totally oblivious to you. Your whole dad thing is deeply riddled with problems and you can't stay with this person who reminds you of him.

ABBY: Maybe you should go to the airport.

CLEA: You are just not staying in fucking London where you can't even be a vegetarian for God's sake. Even Madonna is going home.

ABBY: Okay, first of all Madonna's staying too. Second, this is not your problem. Go home. We'll stay in touch—if you stop saying things that you know nothing about.

CLEA: So, basically, you want to give up your education and your life in New York to be written about? Is that it?

ABBY: You don't get it.

CLEA: Why? Because I'm not pretty enough to be written about?

ABBY: It's not just that.

CLEA: Of course it's not. I was joking.

ABBY: Sorry.

CLEA: Don't be.

ABBY: It has to happen this way.

CLEA: But—

ABBY: I know it's right, I just know.

CLEA: Look. You are abandoning everything that we talked about, everything that I thought you—

ABBY: No, that's just you. I'm abandoning you.

CLEA: No.

ABBY: Bye, Clea. Go home without me. Keep in touch. Visit.

(NICKY *appears at the edges of the space, ready to take the girls to the airport.*)

NICKY: Clea, we really should go.

CLEA: This is what you wanted? This? You just wanted—this—!? I guess I didn't realize—

ABBY: What?

CLEA: That you wanted this.

(*She turns to* NICKY.)

I'm ready.

ABBY: Well, you could say good bye.

CLEA: (*But she can't. To* NICKY—) Let's go.

(CLEA *and* NICKY *leave.* ABBY *stays.*)


### staying

JASON: What about school?

ABBY: Don't you want me to?

JASON: It's not about what I want.

ABBY: So?

JASON: You need to finish school.

ABBY: I don't need to do anything. I choose to stay here with you.

JASON: You can't do that.

ABBY: You need me to write.

JASON: No, I don't.

ABBY: You said you did.

JASON: I was deluded. I'm glad you came though.

ABBY: You motherfucker.

JASON: Abby. It's not like it was. We're not the same. I'm going to be thirty in a few months.

ABBY: So!?

JASON: I needed HER. *(Pointing to the poster)* You're not her.

ABBY: Of course I'm her. I am her. She's me.

JASON: No. She's my creation.

ABBY: You said—

JASON: I know. But I was wrong.

ABBY: I'm me. You wrote about me.

JASON: It's different.

ABBY: I'm her. The girl in your book. Look—

(ABBY *tries to be the girl in the book—she takes the pose of the girl on the poster. This takes a while. Maybe it is awkward for her. She falls out of the picture.*)

JASON: You're not her, Abby. She is a work of fiction. You are a work of... life.

ABBY: I'm her, I'm her, I'm her, I'm her.

JASON: No. You're not. *(He leaves.)*

*(Lights down on everyone.)*

## smashing

JAMES: Which brings us to *Smashing*. My most recent piece of fiction, in which a neophyte first time lucky stiff of a mediocre writer publishes a book about the daughter of his idol, an aging rock star. The daughter declares her love for the young novelist and he rejects her, as young novelists are apt to do, and she comes home. To her father. While the young novelist takes up with assorted unnamed girls whom he later discards. And the daughter, she returns to her father in order to sort out the threads and threats of their past and weave together a future that is eternally now and eternally kaleidoscopic. I was somewhat influenced by something minor that happened to my own daughter, Abby. Who lives in London.

*(Lights up on* ABBY *in London.)*

ABBY: Dear Daddy...
Jason is hard at work on his second book. Still. He's had some troubles. That really sucked about *Cherry, Pie* and how they cast that girl and had to make up all that new dialogue, but he's not taking it too hard, or the reviews either, he's just trying to get through a draft of the new one. It is not called *Roxanne, Roxanne* anymore. I convinced him to change it. I don't know if we'll make it home for Christmas. Things have been... we fight a lot. And I still don't know about finishing school. I just don't know.

### on an airline called virgin

*(*CLEA *reads from her own writing.)*

CLEA: At the end of the summer that she would call "pivotal", "Louise" found herself crossing the ocean on an airline called Virgin. Once this would be an appropriate play on words, but clearly not anymore. Louise thought, I have lost my best friend, and gained an ocean. And new friends who offer to feed me, only it doesn't matter because I am already fed. And it is all just starting. Everything. Now."

## epilogue

*(Lights up on a new young girl-woman, a student. She is fresh and very pretty.)*

GIRL: Dear Mr Stark,
I have just finished reading your wonderful book, and I am writing to you care of your agent, to tell you how deeply and profoundly it moved me. I too feel that I have gone to sleep and your book shocks me awake by taking me to the very depth of the pain of love. I am a college student, although I have seen and felt things that are older than my years. And I am in love with your book. It reminded me of events in my own life, and I just wanted you to know how much I relate to Addie, the girl in your book who is mean to the hero and breaks his heart. I understand this girl. I would love to meet you, Mr Stark, if you are ever in Kansas City. Missouri, not Kansas. I would like to meet you. And talk about your book.

### END OF PLAY

CPSIA information can be obtained
at www.ICGtesting.com
Printed in the USA
LVHW040447030123
736289LV00006B/895

9 780881 454345